BRAIN POWER!

How to ACHIEVE it, how to
INCREASE it, how to USE it.

This is a book that will make you think.

Your brain is the part of you that thinks.
It's the central part of YOU. Because
it's so important to you, you should make
sure it performs as best it can. If you
train it properly, it will be ready to
handle all sorts of tricky situations.
It will solve problems for you, think of
new inventions, generate new ideas, help
you decide what to do in a strange
situation.

This book offers you all sorts of things
to do to get your brain thinking as it's
never thought before. If you tackle
these exercises and problems, BRAIN
POWER can be yours.

**Also by the same author,
and available in Knight Books:**

BRAIN POWER!

Gyles Brandreth

Illustrated by
Mark Hackett

KNIGHT BOOKS
Hodder and Stoughton

First published by Knight Books 1980

Set, printed and bound in Great Britain for
Hodder and Stoughton Paperbacks, a
division of Hodder and Stoughton Ltd.,
Mill Road, Dunton Green, Sevenoaks,
Kent (Editorial Office: 47 Bedford
Square, London, WC1 3DP) by
Cox & Wyman Ltd., Reading

ISBN 0 340 25493 9

Introduction

This is a book for people who have problems. Or who think they have problems. It's also a book for people who don't have any problems right now but who would like to know how to deal with any problems that they might run into.

This is a book that will make you think. And it will make you think in more than just one way. Sometimes problems can't be solved by thinking in one way. Some problems can only be solved by thinking in a new and different way. This book will introduce you to the various ways that you are able to think. Then you will be able to deal with those problems you've got now and the ones that may occur later on.

If you haven't got problems and think that you're not going to get any, perhaps reading this book will help you solve someone else's problems. Running into problems of one sort or another is almost certain to happen. Your friends have problems. Your parents have problems. Your teachers have problems. Other grown-ups have problems. All these people have problems, even if you don't! Of course, they don't all have the same problems. But many of their problems could be tackled if they were thought about in the right way. And this book is going to show you the right ways.

The part of you that thinks is your brain. If you train yourself to use it properly, it can be a wonderful thing. But if you leave it untrained, it isn't always as helpful as it could be.

Your brain is like your legs! Most of the time, your legs manage to do a useful job. You walk up and down stairs. You walk to school. Or you may run to catch a bus or meet a friend. Your legs manage all of these things well enough. But if you wanted to enter for a running race, you would want your legs to do their very best. And that can only be done by training them. Before the race, you would do exercises. And go for runs. You would end up with your legs in a superb condition. Trained well. And ready to win that race.

The same goes for your brain. Most of the time, it manages to muddle along. But every so often, up pops a problem. The problem is really only a problem because your brain doesn't know how to solve it. If it knew how to solve it, it wouldn't be a problem. By training your brain, the problem can be solved.

This book will show you how to use your brain better. How to train it. Make it do exercises. So that it is in the peak of condition when it is time to tackle those problems which you have. Or will have.

This book will give you Brain Power!

Anagrams

An anagram is when you take a word and re-arrange its letters to spell another word. Maybe you start off with LAME. You can rearrange the letters to spell out another word, MEAL. LAME and MEAL are said to be anagrams of each other.

Lots of grown-ups get enjoyment from struggling with anagrams of one sort or another. It's just another form of brain exercise.

If you want to keep your brain agile and nimble, you ought to try some anagrams. Not only will they sharpen your brain, but they might also improve your spelling.

Here are some words that you should know. Can you find an anagram of each one? All the words are quite simple.

Lime. Cats. Seal. Cars. Mary. Bale. Bolt. Care. Diet. East.

And here are some longer ones.

Aches. Eager. Alert. Anger. Boast. Caned. Defer.
Grown. Heart.

(You will find the answers at the back of the book.)

Ask

Sometimes you don't ask questions because you
think you'll look silly. You might be at school and
your teacher is trying to explain something. You
don't really understand it, but everyone else seems
to.

If you're lucky, someone else will ask the questions
instead. But if you're trying to train your brain, you
can't hope that someone else will always ask the
questions that you want answered.

You need to practise asking questions. But you
don't have to start at school. You could begin by
asking friends. Or parents. Or friendly grown-ups.
And you don't have to ask tricky questions. Ask
about things that most people know about. The
idea is not to get the answers. The idea is to give you
practice in asking questions.

Here are some questions that you might like to ask
people.

Why are rooms either square or rectangular?

Why do chairs have four legs?
Why does the earth look flat even though your teacher says it's a globe?
Why do day and night happen?

Asking questions is a good way to find out about something. Asking useful questions is even better. If you ask the right questions, you might find that your problem has gone away.

Here is an exercise that will help you ask useful questions. Imagine that you are an interviewer with your own radio programme. Different people come on your radio show. You want to find out as much as you can about each of the people. But you can only ask each person four questions. What four

9

questions would you ask each person? Remember, you want to find out as much as possible.

Here are the people.

Cinderella.
A teacher who had just been chosen by his class as their favourite teacher.
A grown-up who had just won a fortune in a competition.
The first man to walk on the moon.
A cave-man.
A child your age but born a thousand years ago.
A child your age but born a thousand years in the future.

Backwards

You can probably say the alphabet forwards. But can you say it backwards? You probably know how to spell lots of words. But can you spell them backwards?

Your brain can get stuck in a rut. Saying the alphabet forwards can become so easy that you don't have to think about it. Get your brain out of the rut that it's in. See if you can recite the alphabet backwards. It's not easy, is it?

Make a list of some words that you have learned how to spell at school. Look at each word in turn. Then cover it up. Now spell it backwards. Short words can be quite easy. But can you spell the longer words backwards?

Can you read the sentences in this book backwards? Can you read the sentences on this page backwards? Start at the bottom of the page. Read the words from the end of the line to the beginning of the line. What you are saying won't make sense. But it will be an exercise for your brain.

Can you imagine what would happen if everything in the world happened backwards? People would walk backwards. Motor cars would go backwards. People would get younger instead of older. Every time someone had a birthday, their age would go *down* by one year.

Make a list of all the odd things that would happen. Ask your friends if they can add anything to your list. Ask your teacher, too.

Very strange things would happen if everything went backwards. Thinking about them is certainly a good exercise for your brain.

Both Sides

It's easy to look at something. It is what it is. And that's what you see.

Be careful. Your brain might be stuck in a rut. It might be stopping you from exploring alternatives.

Take an empty pint glass. Put half a pint of water in it. Now, is the glass *half-full*? Or is it *half-empty*?

When you leave home in the morning to go to school, what do you really do? Do you walk *away* from home? Or do you walk *to* school?

Your mother sends you on an errand to the grocer's shop. You want to buy some sugar. And some bread. And some brown eggs. But the lady in the shop says they haven't got any brown eggs. Why? Have they sold them all? Or doesn't the shop ever sell brown eggs?

Do the walls of a house hold the roof in place? Or does the roof keep the walls from falling down?

Imagine that you are in a park on a summer day. The sun is shining brightly. The sky is bright blue. You feel hot. It's a hot day. Now imagine that you are from Africa, where the sun beats down for a lot of the time. Would you feel just as hot in the park? Would it still be a hot day? Or would it be chilly

compared with what you were used to? The sun might be shining. The sky might be bright blue. But you might feel cold. Who is to say whether it is a hot day or not?

Take care that your brain doesn't get stuck in a rut. There can often be two ways of considering a situation. Or even more. Just because you can see one way, don't assume that it is the only one. Look for other ways of seeing things. Of thinking about situations. Flex your brain. Make it consider all the angles.

Try this one. When you look into a mirror, your left hand has become your right hand. And your right hand has become your left hand. The mirror has reversed your image from left to right. Have you ever wondered why it doesn't also reverse your image from top to bottom? Why doesn't your head appear near the floor? And why don't your feet appear where your head normally does? Maybe you haven't thought about it before. So think about it now.

Be careful not to take things for granted. Consider all the angles.

Brain

This is what you are trying to exercise.

Your brain is in your head. At the top of your head. It's what makes the rest of your body work. It's the part that tells the legs to walk. And the arms to swing. And the lips to whistle. It's also the part of you which thinks. Which has ideas. Which works out problems. Which decides about things. The brain is the central part of you.

Because it's so important to you, you should make sure that it performs as best it can. There are all sorts of things that the brain can do, but doesn't often do. If you can train it to do these things, it will be ready to handle all sorts of tricky situations. It will let you solve problems, think of new inventions, generate new ideas, think up new songs, remember old songs, help you decide what to do in a strange situation.

This book offers you all sorts of things to do to get your brain thinking as it's never thought before. If you can tackle these exercises and problems, Brain Power can be yours.

C

Colours

Colours are interesting things to think about. They are a good way of getting your brain to think about something.

Make a list of as many colours as you can think of. As well as the obvious ones like red and blue, think of some more unusual ones. Now close your eyes. Try to imagine each of the colours in turn. Try to imagine one colour fading into the next colour. You might be able to close your eyes and imagine yellow. And you might be able to imagine purple. But can you imagine the change from yellow to purple? That's a bit harder than just imagining the colours by themselves.

See if you can think of things that go with each of the colours on your list. You ought to find it easy to think of things that are blue. Or red. Or yellow. But purple might be a bit harder. And orange, too. Try to think of things that are blends of different colours. Can you think of anything that is a bluey orange? Or a greeny purple? Or brilliant pink?

What is your favourite colour? Or colours? Can you say why? What are your friends' favourite colours? It might be interesting to ask everyone in your class what their favourite colour is and why. Do you think that they would all pick different colours? Or would they all pick the same colour? Do some colours get mentioned more often than others? Do some colours never get mentioned? Can you work out why this is?

Do you think that people connect different colours with different things? Does everyone connect blue with blue skies and sunny days? Does everyone connect green with being outdoors, near to a park or field? Does everyone connect red with fire? And what do people connect with black? And mauve? And pink?

Connections

A problem may often seem like a jumble of unrelated smaller problems. But the smaller problems might be connected with each other. Only you haven't realised it.

Look for connections between things. If you can see how to deal with one problem, perhaps you will be able to deal with another problem if it is connected.

Your brain doesn't always look for connections. Make it. Lots of things don't seem to be connected when you first consider them. Think about them for a while longer. Connections often do appear.

Try this exercise. Here is a list of 16 things. They don't seem to have much to do with each other.

cat	television	pen	car
carpet	garden	bread	farm
cowboy	teapot	nurse	chimney
dustbin	tennis	fire	plasticine

Choose any two of the words. Try to think of a link. What do they have in common? See if you can think of a second link. And a third one.

Then try the exercise with any other two words. Can they be linked? Can they be linked in more than just one way?

Try the same exercise on your friends. Or your brothers and sisters, if you have any. Or your parents. Compare your answers with theirs. Are they the same? Or different? If they are different, do you understand how they have arrived at their connections?

There are no *right* answers. This kind of thinking can be useful when dealing with a problem. Seeing the connection between two or more things might be just what is needed to solve the problem. Or make it easier to manage.

Daft Ideas

Even daft ideas can be useful, especially when you begin to understand why an idea seems so daft.

If an idea is daft, that should prepare you for the way other people will look on it. If it really is totally and completely daft, perhaps you had better keep quiet about it!

What is it that makes an idea, or a statement, or a question daft? Or silly? Or just plain nonsense?

Here are some silly statements. But can you decide why they are daft? If you've really got your wits about you, you might think of good reasons why they *aren't* daft!

Red is a thicker colour than brown.
Z is a funnier letter than P.
Cement is juicier than a sack of feathers.
A cough is more munchy than a sneeze.
A snowflake is taller than a chuckle.

Can you see what makes each of these silly?

Here are four sentences. Read them through first and then read what comes after them.

Green ideas sleep furiously.
Elastic thoughts snooze widely.
Strangely curtains purple grunt.
Aeroplanes banana-shaped softly mumble.

The first two of these are silly. They read like sentences, but don't make proper sense. The second two are sillier still. They don't even read like sentences. They are just jumbles of words.

Can you see this difference between the first two and the last two? Try composing silly sentences of your own, like the first two. They must read like sentences, but just not make true sense.

Deductions

A deduction is something that you work out for yourself. If you are given two facts, you might be able to deduce (or work out) a third fact from them.

Here is an example:

It always rains on Tuesdays.
It is not raining today.

From these two facts, you should be able to work out that today is not a Tuesday. Do you get the idea? You were told the first two facts. But you worked out a third fact from them. That's a deduction.

Just to make sure that you've got the hang of these deductions, here are some more:-

All wasps are unfriendly.
All unfriendly creatures are horrible.

Can you deduce from these two facts that all wasps are horrible?

No medicine is nice.
Cough mixture is a medicine.

From these two facts, can you deduce that cough mixture isn't nice?

People with Brain Power are clever.
You have Brain Power.

The deduction that you should be able to make from these two facts is that you are clever! But you probably knew that all along, didn't you?

Now here are some for you to try by yourself. Some are true; some are not!

Kevin is a hard working boy.
All hard working people are happy.

Some dreams are terrible.
All dreams are in colour.

All my sisters have colds.
No-one can sing who has a cold.

No grown-ups are patient.
No impatient person can sit still.

No four-legged animals can whistle.
All cats have four legs.

(You will find the answers at the back of the book.)

Descriptions

How good are you at describing things? If you describe things in a vague muddled way, it's because your brain isn't pulling its weight. See if you can give short accurate descriptions of these objects:

jug	telephone	bicycle	teeth
spiral	window	food mixer	tyre
staircase	shoe-laces	comb	tablecloth
chimney	glasses	doormat	circus
satchel			

Would your descriptions be understood by someone who had never come across these objects before?

Would they make sense to someone from Mars? Assuming they could speak English, of course!

Try your descriptions on your friends. Can they guess the objects you are describing? If not, what's wrong with your descriptions?

The Dictionary

This is a game that will help you in several ways. It will give you practice at using a dictionary: looking for words in it, and reading their definitions. It will also help you to learn how other people think.

To play this game, you need at least three people, some paper, a pencil for each player, and a dictionary. A school dictionary will do. Or your parents' dictionary. Or your own dictionary if you have one.

Here are the rules. One person looks in the dictionary and finds a word that none of the players knows. There will be lots to choose from, because dictionaries contain lots of unusual words. The person announces the word to the other players.

Each of the players invents a possible definition of the word and writes it down. The person with the dictionary writes down the real definition. If the word has more than one definition in the dictionary, any one of the definitions will do.

All the definitions go to the person with the dictionary. That person then reads out all the definitions, including the real one. The players then have to guess which is the correct definition.

Suppose that the word chosen was 'drake'. Which of these is the right definition?

A small river.
A male duck.
A garden tool.
A fish.

Choose one of these, and then check the dictionary.

Keep score like this. When a person chooses the right definition, he scores one point. A person scores one point each time the other players choose his definition.

The dictionary person changes each time the game is played.

Here's what to look for. Which players are choosing the right definitions a lot? And which players aren't getting many right at all? Which players are writing definitions that get chosen a lot? What does this tell you about the people playing? Does it tell you something new, something that you didn't know before? Or does it tell you something that you already knew?

Differences

Can you figure out the differences between the various things mentioned here? Remember that these are trick questions and the answer in each case is a play on words.

What's the difference between a china shop and a furniture shop?

What's the difference between a train driver and a school teacher?

What's the difference between an elephant and a flea?

What's the difference between killed soldiers and torn clothes that have been repaired?

What's the difference between a boxer and a man with a cold?

What's the difference between a silly rabbit and a fake coin?

What's the difference between a fisherman and a lazy student?

What's the difference between a glutton and a hungry man?

What's the difference between a hill and a pill?

(You will find the answers at the back of the book.)

Dotto

This is a brain-teasing game for two, three or four players. What you will need is a large sheet of paper and a pencil.

The first player writes the number 1 anywhere on the sheet of paper. And places a dot next to it.

The second player writes the number 2 anywhere on the sheet of paper. And places a dot next to it.

Players continue in this way until they reach the number 20. By this time, there will be twenty numbers and twenty dots on the paper.

Now the first player connects the dot next to the number 1 with the dot next to the number 2. He can use a straight line, or a curved line, or a wiggly line. It doesn't matter.

The next player connects the dot next to the number 2 with the dot next to the number 3. Any sort of line can be drawn.

The players carry on in this way, always connecting up the next dot. Players should try to make sure that the lines they draw don't touch or cross other lines unless they really have to.

The scores are kept like this.

If a player touches or crosses a line, he scores one point. If a player touches or crosses two lines, he scores two points. And so on. If a player draws a line through any dots except the two he is trying to connect, he scores two points. If a player draws a line through a place where two other lines cross, he scores two points.

The winner is the player with the *lowest* score at the end.

There are several different ways that this game can be played. You might like to try them.

Instead of using all the numbers from 1 to 20, you might use just the even numbers from 2 to 40. The even numbers go 2, 4, 6, 8, 10, 12, and so on.

You might like to use bigger numbers and more of them. The numbers could go from 101 to 150. In this case, you would have fifty dots.

You might like to use *any* twenty numbers between 1 and 100. Players then have to connect them up in order. They could go 1, 4, 12, 13, 23, 29, and so on.

Drawing

Once in a while, a dog needs to be let off its lead to have a good run; the same goes for your brain. It needs to think silly thoughts. Crazy ideas. Weird images. Brain waves. And fanciful points of view. Grown-ups call this 'brain storming'. Every so often, a good idea will emerge. And all the silly ones can be forgotten. Try your own brain storming exercise.

Make a mental list of all the things which the world needs. A rain-making machine. A machine to blow away fog. A machine to stop cars having accidents. A machine to make your bed in the morning. A machine to retrieve your ball when it goes over a neighbour's wall. And so on.

Now try drawing these things. How would they work? How big would they be? Or how small? Would they need wheels? What about switches? You might end up drawing something that could work. Show it to your friends. Do they think it would work? If not, why wouldn't it work? Perhaps you can improve your design. All the best inventors worked on their inventions for a long time. More than one inventor could be involved where the invention was particularly large or difficult. Make some changes to your drawing. Would that work? Ask your parents or a teacher.

The inventor of television didn't just sit down one day and invent television. It took a long time. Years, even. At first, the pictures were very small. And they weren't very clear. And they were in black and white. Not colour. Even when a thing has been invented, it can always be improved.

Think of lots of objects from your home that could be improved. If there is a refrigerator, how could it be improved? And what changes could be made to the furniture? Perhaps the furniture needs to be light so that it can be moved easily. Perhaps it needs to be strong if you are going to climb all over it. Perhaps it should be easier to keep clean. How could these improvements be made?

Again, draw pictures of your improvements. Show them to your parents. Listen to any objections that your parents may have. Then go away and improve on the improvements!

E

Ends

With some problems, it's not the answer that's the problem. You know what the answer is. What you don't know is how to get to it. That's the problem.

There may be several ways of getting to the answer. It may only be necessary to find one of those several ways. Most satisfying of all is to find the best way.

Quite often, working backwards from the answer is simpler than working forwards to the answer. Imagine the situation described here.

There are six fishermen sitting on the bank of a river. Each has got a fishing rod. All the lines have got tangled up. At the end of one of the lines is a fish. The other lines have nothing on their ends. Which fisherman has caught the fish?

Tracing from the fishing rods might give you the answer in one go. But it might take as many as six goes. Much better would be to follow the line from the fish's end. Having traced the line, you will find out which fisherman has caught the fish.

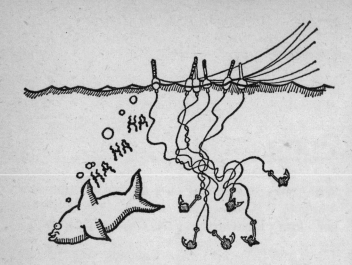

Now think about this one. Get six empty glasses. Stand them in a straight line. Put some water into the first three glasses, leaving the last three empty still. You may touch and move only one glass. Now what you have to do is this: change the arrangement so that no empty glass is next to another empty glass and no glass with water in is next to another glass with water in.

Can you see how to do it? If not, it might help to get six more glasses. Arrange them in a straight line in the way that you know they have got to end up. Comparing the two rows of glasses should suggest something. You will see that the water in the second glass has got to get into the fifth glass. You can transfer the water by pouring! No-one said pouring wasn't allowed!

By starting at the end, you have discovered the solution. The problem is solved. Not every problem can be solved like this. But lots can. Get your brain to look at problems from the other end. It might just help.

Exercises

When a part of your body moves, it's because the brain has told it to do so. Even physical exercises involve the brain.

If you were to run on the spot, without moving backwards or forwards, the brain is involved. The brain is telling your legs to lift themselves off the ground. It's telling your knees to bend. And it's telling your legs to put themselves back on the ground. The brain is also making sure that you don't have both feet off the ground at the same time, otherwise you would topple over! The brain is also making sure that you run on the spot rather than run backwards or forwards. It is telling your legs that you are to stay where you are.

The aim of this book is not to build up your muscles. It is to build up your brain. To get it into the peak of condition. You are not going to have to run on the spot. You are not going to have to do exhausting exercises, but you are going to have to move certain parts of your body. You won't find it too difficult to move your tongue, will you?

Stick out your tongue as far as you can, keeping it straight. Concentrate. Push it right out. Then slide it back into your mouth as far as it will go. Repeat this ten times.

Now stick out your tongue to try and touch your nose. Repeat this ten times.

Stick out your tongue to try and touch your chin. Repeat this ten times.

Put the tip of your tongue on your upper lip. Run the tip round your lips in a clockwise direction. Do this ten times. Then stop. Now run the tip of your tongue round your lips ten times in the opposite direction.

All these exercises are to make you concentrate on a part of your body. There's no reason why you shouldn't be able to do any of these simple exercises. Because you don't tackle them everyday, you may have to concentrate quite hard to do them properly. In the end, it's your brain which is being exercised.

Now close your eyes. Hold your right hand out in front of your body as far as you can. Keep your eyes closed. Move your right hand towards your face so that the tip of your thumb touches the end of your nose. Did you miss it slightly? Keep your eyes closed. Do the same thing with each of the finger-tips on your right hand. Then repeat the exercise with your left thumb and fingers. Are certain fingers more accurate than others at locating the tip of your nose? If so, why do you think that is?

F

Favourites

If you like something, do you know why? If not, try and think why.

Make a list of your favourite things. Your favourite food. Your favourite television programme. Your favourite teacher. Your favourite day of the week. Your favourite book. Your favourite colour. Your favourite drink. You can probably think of lots more favourites to add to this list.

Can you say why each of your favourites really is your favourite? Why do you really prefer one food to another? Is it the taste that's nicer? Or the feel of the food in your mouth? Or is the smell more pleasant? Try and work out why. Why is one teacher your favourite and not another? What does your favourite let you do that the other doesn't? If Saturday is your favourite day, why? Why not Sunday? Or one of the weekdays?

It's one thing to be able to say you like something. It's so much better when you can say *why* you like it.

Fizz~Buzz

This is a game called Fizz-Buzz. Some people call it Buzz-Fizz. And others call it just Buzz. But here, it will be called Fizz-Buzz. It will exercise your brain and help it work quickly.

You need at least two people to play the game. More people can play if you want them to.

The idea of the game is to count from 1 to as high as you possibly can, without ever mentioning a 5 or a multiple of 5. Numbers like 10, 15, 20, 25, 30 and 35 are called multiples of 5, because you can divide 5 into them without getting a remainder. Not only must you not mention 5 and its multiples, you mustn't mention 7 and its multiples. The multiples of 7 are numbers like 14, 21, 28, 35, 42 and 49, because you can divide 7 into them without getting a remainder.

Instead of saying a 5 or a multiple of 5, you must say 'Fizz!' Instead of saying a 7 or a multiple of 7, you must say 'Buzz!' Now you can see why the game's called Fizz-Buzz.

Anyone who makes a mistake drops out. And making a mistake can be mentioning a 5 or a multiple of 5 or a 7 or a multiple of 7. Or saying 'Fizz!' when they should have said 'Buzz!' Or saying

'Buzz!' when they should have said 'Fizz!' Or saying anything ridiculous like 'Buzz buzz!' or 'Fizz buzz!' or 'Fuzz bizz!'

Here's a quick example from two friends, Pinky and Perky, to give you the general idea.

Pinky: 1.
Perky: 2.
Pinky: 3.
Perky: 4.
Pinky: Fizz!
Perky: 6.
Pinky: Buzz!
Perky: 8.
Pinky: 9.
Perky: Fizz!
Pinky: 11.
Perky: 12.
Pinky: 13.
Perky: Buzz!
Pinky: Fizz!
Perky: 14.

Whoops! Perky should have said 16, not 14. Perky drops out. And Pinky becomes the winner.

Friends

It's nice to have friends. That's why they are friends. Friends are there to play with. To talk to. To do things with. And sometimes friends might even help with your problems. Or you might want to help a friend with one of their problems.

How well do you know your friends? What facts do you know about them? Do you know their ages? And the colour of their eyes? Do you know how tall they are? Taller or shorter than you? Do you know whether they have brothers and sisters? Do you know the names of the brothers and sisters? Have you been to their homes? Can you describe their homes? What else do you know about your friends? Do you know their favourite things? And where they went on holiday? And what their fathers' and/or mothers' jobs are?

Perhaps you don't know all these facts about your friends. But you must know some things about them. Or else they wouldn't be your friends.

Some friends are useful to have around when you have a problem. Some friends will help you think about the problem. Others won't be much use, though. Some friends will say whatever they think you want to hear. Other friends will just make silly suggestions. Which friends are more helpful when you have problems? Try and learn something from the way they tackle the problem. Which friends aren't helpful? Why aren't they?

If you think about your friends like this, you will have a much clearer idea of who to turn to when the next problem occurs. If you want help, you won't go to those friends who are just going to get you nowhere.

Games

There are lots of games in this book. Games are important in developing Brain Power. Games are also fun.

All games have rules. You have to understand the rules of a game before you can play it. And learning how a game is played can be wonderful exercise for your brain.

Even if you think that the rules of a particular game are silly, it's still good practice for your brain to try to stay within the rules.

Suppose you're playing a card game. As you know, cards are clubs or diamonds or hearts or spades. Your brain may never have come across a club or a spade before. But before too long, it can tell the difference. And it soon learns to tell the jack, queen and king apart. Games are full of new and novel things for your brain to cope with.

Of course, some people like winning at games even

more than just playing them. But ask yourself: should you play a game just to win? Or just to enjoy it? Or should you try to do both at the same time?

Try and think of all the different games that you have ever played. Ball games. Card games. Skipping games. Games with matches. Games with dominoes. I-spy games. Guessing games. Games with boards. You can probably think of lots.

What about games that you've heard of but haven't played? Make a list of them. Why haven't you played them? Try and find out how to play them. Ask your friends. Ask your teachers. If there's a grown-ups' game that you'd like to learn, ask your parents.

H

Hearing

What can you hear? Sit still. See how many different things you can hear, however faintly. There might be a clock ticking. And a car going past outside. And the wind whistling in the trees. And there goes a train. And there's a bird singing. And you can hear a fire engine's siren somewhere in the distance.

Try this at different times of day. And in different places. Even lying in bed at night, you ought to be able to hear a lot of different noises, though they may be quite faint.

How good are you at identifying different noises? Try this exercise. You'll need a friend to help you. One of you closes your eyes. The other one makes a sound with something that happens to be in the room, or outdoors, or wherever you are. One idea is to tap a pencil on the table. Another is to rustle a newspaper. You can probably think of lots more. Take turns, each of you trying to catch the other out.

As time goes on, do you get better? Is your sense of hearing improving? Were some sounds easy for you both? Or difficult for you both? Were they similar sorts of sounds? Or were they very different?

Help!

You may have a problem. You might want to be alone to think about it. Or you might want to be with friends. Or your teacher. Or other grown-ups. It's not always easy to ask these people for help.

Some friends (and some grown-ups) will always agree with you. They like you a lot. They don't want you to feel upset. So they end up agreeing with whatever you say. They may tell you not to worry. That the problem will disappear soon. Ask yourself, is that sort of help always the best sort?

Some people will have the solution straightaway. They tell you what to do. Even if their suggested solution works, is that the best thing? Have they helped you to think about your problem?

Some people are lots of fun. Always laughing, and joking, and playing around. That's great. But you don't want them to behave like that when you are trying to explain your problem to them.

And some people like to talk, and talk, and talk. You start off trying to explain your problem. But you don't get too far. They start replying. And they just go on talking, and talking, and talking. Somehow you feel that the problem has got lost somewhere beneath all the talk.

Think about the sort of help you want from people. Then think about the people you know and how they would respond. Try to match up the sort of help you want with the people you know.

How?

There are lots of questions that begin with the word HOW. Here are a few. Try them on your friends and teachers. They will all have different ways of answering the questions. Some may manage to give a short interesting answer. Others might not know the answer at all, but talk as if they do know. Others might know the answer, but take ages to actually tell it to you.

Here are the questions.

How do clouds produce rain?
How does a telephone work?
How are books printed?
How do people forecast the weather?

How does a fish breathe underwater?
How did sandy beaches come to be made?

Perhaps you can think of lots more HOW questions
of your own. Try those on your friends and teachers, too.

Ideas

All the best thinkers have ideas. Ideas for new inventions. Ideas for new ways of doing things. Ideas for new games. Ideas for better ways of doing things. Let's see if you can come up with an idea. It could be a completely new idea. Or it could be an idea that's been floating around in the back of your mind for a while.

Tell your idea to various friends, but not when they are all together. Tell them separately. And tell the idea seriously.

See how people react to your idea. Are they polite? Are they prepared to listen? Are they prepared to help? Do they offer lots of reasons why your idea won't work? Or is a bad one?

How people react may tell you something about your idea. If everyone thinks it's a wonderful idea, then it could be. (Are you really sure that they are not all telling you that just to keep you happy?) If everyone thinks that it's a rotten idea, then the chances are that it is. But ask yourself: Are these people really capable of fully understanding the idea?

You could try out two ideas. One that really is good. And one that you know is silly. It will be interesting to see what they have to say about the silly idea. It could tell you quite a lot about the people you are asking.

Imagine

An important part of brain stimulation is using all of your senses. Elsewhere in *Brain Power* there are exercises concerned with seeing, and listening, and touching, but this is an exercise in imagining that you are doing various things with your senses.

Lots of people have problems in imagining things. They could do it if they tried. But they would find it easier to do if they had started using their imagination when they were younger. Like lots of other activities, learning to do something new becomes more difficult as you get older.

Try to imagine the things below. Is each one easy? Or hard? Or totally impossible?

Imagine the smell of petrol.

Imagine the smell of Marmite.
Imagine the smell of bacon and eggs.
Imagine the smell of cheese and onion crisps.
Imagine the smell of fresh paint.
Imagine the smell of new-mown grass.
Imagine the smell of a wet dog.

Now for some more complicated exercises involving imaginary smells. Try to imagine these.

Imagine the smell of a banana changing into the smell of an orange.
Imagine the smell of burnt toast changing into the smell of tomato ketchup.
Imagine the smell of perfume changing into the smell of coffee.
Imagine the smell of chips changing into the smell of a bonfire.

Imagine the smell of lemonade changing into the smell of your Sunday dinner.
Imagine the smell of sawdust changing into the smell of cigarette smoke.

How did you manage with those? They should have been harder than the first lot of imaginary smelling exercises.

Your sense of smell and your sense of taste are closely related. Try imagining the tastes of different things. Are the following ones easy? Or hard? Or totally impossible?

Imagine the taste of vanilla ice cream.
Imagine the taste of sausages.
Imagine the taste of strawberries.
Imagine the taste of the nastiest medicine you know.
Imagine the taste of chocolate.
Imagine the taste of orange juice.
Imagine the taste of a boiled egg (the yellow *and* white parts).

Here are some complicated exercises involving imaginary tastes. See how well you get on with these.

Imagine the taste of cheese changing into the taste of tea.
Imagine the taste of toffees changing into the taste of water.
Imagine the taste of fish fingers changing into the taste of custard.
Imagine the taste of an apple changing into the taste of rhubarb.
Imagine the taste of a tomato changing into the taste of sardines.
Imagine the taste of chocolate digestive biscuits changing into the taste of milk.
Imagine the taste of sugar changing into the taste of brown bread.

Tricky? Or perhaps they were quite easy?

Enough of smells and tastes! Now it's time for you to imagine the feel of various things. Different materials have different feels. Some are smooth. Some are rough. Some always feel cold. Others always feel warm. See if you can imagine all the sensations when you feel the following things.

Imagine the feel of a woollen jumper.
Imagine the feel of a wet piece of soap.
Imagine the feel of a handful of sand.
Imagine the feel of a brick.
Imagine the feel of an over-ripe tomato.
Imagine the feel of glass.
Imagine the feel of a slice of bread.
Imagine the feel of a slice of toast.

How did you get on? Were some easier than others? Very few people get the chance to imagine different things like these. Their imaginations wither and become useless. Problem solvers need fertile imaginations. You need a fertile imagination. It all adds to your brain power!

I~Spy

You probably know the game of I-Spy. One player says 'I spy with my little eye something beginning with the letter ...' The other players then have to try and guess what object it is that the first player has chosen.

In this version of I-Spy, you don't have to have the assistance of other players. You can play all by yourself.

Decide on a letter of the alphabet. Perhaps, B. Then look around you. Make a list of all the things beginning with B. You might see a bed, a bath, a bag, a basket, a bread board, a book, a bacon sandwich, a box of chocolates, and so on. When you've exhausted (really, really exhausted) the objects beginning with that letter, choose another one. Repeat the exercise with as many letters as you wish.

You don't have to choose a letter. You could choose a colour. And then you could look for things having that colour.

Or you could look for things that were less than a metre from the ground. Or things that were made of wood. Or things that had plastic parts.

There's no end to the number of different properties you could look for. And the game can work indoors just as well as outdoors. You'll find it improves your observation, which, in turn, adds to your brain power!

J

Jobs

A boy went to the dentist to have his aching tooth seen to. The boy was the dentist's son, but the dentist was not the boy's father. How come?

This is a straightforward question. No tricks. The boy really was the son of the dentist. If the dentist wasn't the boy's father, then it must have been his mother!

This is only a problem because there are more men dentists than women dentists, so you probably pictured a man rather than a woman. That's just another example of the type of blinkered thinking that you must learn to get rid of.

Once upon a time, only men would have been dentists. But these days, lots of women become dentists. And bus drivers. And lorry drivers. And vets. In the past, it was only women who became nurses. But nowadays, it isn't difficult to find nurses who are men. Some men become secretaries.

Preconceived ideas about what sorts of jobs people may have prove that your brain is in a rut. Ideas about certain jobs only being done by men or only by women show that it's in a rut, too. Get it out of that rut. Don't keep falling into traps!

Make two lists of jobs. One list is to contain all the jobs that you would like to do. The other list is to contain all the jobs that you would hate to do. Which list is the larger? What does that tell you about yourself?

Jokes

Exercising your brain is a serious business. So what have jokes got to do with brain power?

You must know lots of jokes. Think of one of them. Consider it carefully. What makes it a joke? Why is it funny? Is it because it has an unexpected ending? Does it present a very strange situation? What does it have that amused you and made you laugh?
'Why does Father Christmas always go down the chimney?'
'Because it soots him!'

'What's the best thing to put in pies?'
'Teeth!'

'What holds the moon up?'
'Moon-beams.'

'What kind of jam cannot be eaten?'
'A traffic jam.'

Can you see what it is that makes each of these jokes a joke? Even if you don't find them that funny, someone else will do. What makes other people laugh at jokes?

Jumbles

How keen an eye have you got? Even when you are told that something's there, can you still spot it? Even when it's surrounded by lots of other things to distract you.

Here is what looks like a jumble of letters.

D O V E M U W

X W H A W K O

E L E G N R L

C F N L N A L

R W R E N L A

O N A W S I W

W O R R A P S

The names of twelve different birds have been hidden in this jumble of letters. The names of the birds can be read out from left to right. Or right to left. Or top to bottom. Or bottom to top.

The birds included in the jumble are these.

Crow, dove, eagle, emu, hawk, hen, lark, owl, sparrow, swallow, swan, wren.

How long did it take you to find all the birds?

Here's the same sort of jumble. But much bigger. This one contains the names of lots of animals. How long will it take you to spot all of the animals?.

```
B E A R H I N O X N C O
P L I O N D E E R F H E
Y E K N O D R A P O E L
E P E E H S G I U T E G
C H O R S E O O M T T I
T A O G I P R N A E A R
Z N P R E M I Y S R H A
E T P E L R L E L A O F
B X I G U E L K T E E F
R C H I M P A N Z E E E
A P E T I O D O G T R S
W O C E S U O M N P A L
```

The animals included in this jumble are these.

Ape, bear, cheetah, chimpanzee, cow, deer, dog, donkey, elephant, elk, foal, giraffe, goat, gorilla, hippo, horse, leopard, lion, monkey, mouse, mule, otter, ox, pig, puma, rhino, sheep, tiger, zebra.

Why not make up your own jumbles and try them on your friends?

Knowledge

A famous writer called Thomas Carlyle once wrote 'What is all knowledge but recorded experience?' What do you think he meant by that?

What he meant was that every piece of knowledge has to be discovered. Nothing is knowledge until someone has worked it out for himself. Someone has to experience something before they can pass it on to other people as knowledge.

Everyone knows that the world is round. It's a great big large globe that goes round the Sun. But once upon a time, people didn't know this. A few people suspected it might be round, but nearly everyone else thought it was flat. They thought that if you went too close to the edge you would drop off. To prove that the world was round, someone actually sailed right round the world in a ship. That person's experience then became everyone else's knowledge. Sailing round the world was a very brave thing to do when everyone was predicting that you might fall off the edge!

59

Lots of athletes can run a mile in less than four minutes. But not so long ago, everyone thought it was impossible. It wasn't until one man did it, or experienced it, that it became knowledge that a mile could be run in less than four minutes.

There are lots of other examples. Every fact, every piece of knowledge, has to be experienced by someone before it becomes knowledge.

All the things that people now know were unknown once upon a time. All these things had to be experienced by some people. These people passed them on to their friends and children. Their experiences became everyone else's knowledge!

Everything that you know is a result of other people's experiences or your own experiences.

L

Letters

Ordinary printed words are reversed when seen in a mirror. It doesn't matter whether you write them across the page or down the page. Try these two in a mirror:

<pre>
                    P
                    O
      BRAIN   W
                    E
                    R
</pre>

But there are some words which do read the same way on the page and in the mirror. Hold these up to a mirror and see:

<pre>
A   H   M   M   T   T   T   W
U   O   O   Y   A   O   O   H
T   O   U   T   X   M   O   A
O   T   U   H   I   A   T   M
              T   T   H
                                   O
</pre>

Why does this work for these words but not for others?

Some words won't work like this if they are written down the page. But they will work if they are written across the page. Here are some that do work:

CHECKED CHOICE DECK   DICE
DOCKED ECHO   HOOKED   KICKED

But even these ones work only if the page is properly held up to a mirror. Can you work out how the page has to be held?

(If you can't work it out, you'll find out how to do it at the back of the book.)

Without stopping to count them, how many letters of the alphabet (when written as capital letters) have curves in them? And how many are made up of just straight lines? Now go through the alphabet carefully and see if you were right.

These few exercises involving letters are to try and get your brain limbered up. To stop it from seeing words and letters in boring old predictable ways. There is always more than one way of looking at something.

Lists

Making lists is another way in which you can get to grips with a problem. Or whatever else it may be that is puzzling you, or perplexing you. Lots of people make lists to help them get jobs done and in the right order. Your Mum probably makes out a shopping list. If she didn't, she'd have a problem remembering all the things she wanted when she got to the shops. People make lists at Christmas time to help them remember who they have to send Christmas cards to. You probably make lists at Christmas and your birthday, indicating what presents you would like to receive.

Another use for lists is to help you think, by looking at things in different ways.

Here are some list exercises. You can do the exercises by yourself. But doing them with a friend can be more fun. You can compare lists.

List all the foods that you can think of that are pink.
List all the ball games you can think of.
List all the teachers in your school.
List all your uncles, aunts, and other grown-up relations.
List all the television programmes that you can think of.

While you are making your lists, you ought to be noticing something. How did your lists begin? After you'd written down all the easy ones, how did you go on to tackle the harder ones? What did you do? How did you decide that you had come to the end of a list? What told you that you had finished?

Now make a list of your problems, if you have any. Is there a teacher at school that you don't like? Is there work at school that you have difficulty in understanding? Do you not like sleeping in the dark? Does your Mum make you eat tomato soup that you don't like? Write down all your problems. Then try and put them in order. Which are the really important ones? And which ones are minor, not really causing too much trouble? Work out why the important ones are important. And why the others are not so important.

Logic

Be logical. Think logically. Use logic and you can't go wrong. Logic never fails. That's the sort of thing that people keep saying.

But what is logic? How does it work? Does it always work? Or does it sometimes give silly answers? Or even the wrong answers?

Here's how logic works. You begin by picking a direction for your thinking to go in. Then you proceed step by step. You check that each step along the way makes sense. If it does, you go on to the next step. You check that, and continue. Eventually, you should arrive at the solution or answer to whatever the problem was.

Ah! But how do you pick the direction to go in at the start? Good question. Somehow you need a push. If you get a push in the wrong direction, then logic will lead you to the wrong solution. And if you don't get any push at all to begin with, logic won't take you anywhere at all!

A bar of chocolate can last forever, logically. All

you have to do is eat just a half of it at a time. Start off by eating half the chocolate. Then put it away. The next time you feel hungry, eat half of what's left. Then put it away. When you're next hungry, eat half of what's left. Carry on eating half of what's left every time you get hungry.

Logically, you will never finish the chocolate. There will always be some left to eat half of.

The problem is that the amount that gets left is getting smaller and smaller. Every time you eat half of what's left, you are getting a smaller and smaller amount of chocolate. After the first few bites, the size of the bites has become so small that it seems pointless to continue.

When you arrive at a solution logically, look at it again. Is it reasonable? Does it make sense? The chocolate bar problem has been solved logically. But you can see that there is little sense in eating tiny little bits of chocolate.

When a logical approach does work, great! When it doesn't, you'll have to try something else.

Here is a logical exercise which ought to work out okay. Suppose that there are only two sorts of animal that have long ears. Donkeys and rabbits. Suppose that there are only two sorts of animal that have long tails. Donkeys and horses. Now suppose that you come across an animal with long ears and a long tail. What must it be?

Here's the same sort of problem, but involving un-familiar animals. Only two sorts of animal have purple lips. Grumpers and snouters. And only two sorts of animal have no ears. Snouters and snifflers.

Now suppose you come across an animal which has purple lips and no ears. What sort is it?

Looking

How much of what you have looked at lately have you ignored? Has your brain ignored? Your brain has been letting you down. You've been looking at various things. But your brain just hasn't bothered to register them all. Or even most of them.

How much has it overlooked lately?

Try this little quiz. See what your brain has chosen to ignore, perhaps sensibly, perhaps not.

Answer each of these questions 'true' or 'false'.

The turntable on a record player goes round in a clockwise direction.
Your bedroom door opens in toward your bedroom.
Page 38 of this book is a left-hand page.
The stripes on a zebra's legs are horizontal.
There are more girls than boys in your class.

You always put on your left shoe before your right shoe.

On coins, the Queen's head faces left.

On stamps, the Queen's head faces left.

Which ones were you sure about? And which did you guess at? Try the questions again in a week's time. See which answers your brain has stored and which ones it has forgotten during the week.

Magic Squares

There are lots of people who like playing around with numbers. They love numbers.

These people would be amused by this arrangement of numbers:

1	15	10	8
14	4	5	11
7	9	16	2
12	6	3	13

In fact, they would be so amused by this square that they would call it a Magic Square.

What's special about it, you might think.

If you add up the numbers in each row, they all add up to 34. And if you add up the numbers in each column, they all add up to 34. And if you add up the numbers going from the top left corner to the bottom right corner, the total is 34. And if you add up the numbers going from the top right corner to the bottom left corner, they add up to 34. Amazing!

Magic squares aren't easy to make up, but it's fun to have a go.

Here's a partly finished magic square. See if you can work out what the missing numbers are.

(You will find the missing numbers at the back of the book.)

Magic Word Squares

Just as there are lots of people who like to play with numbers, there are lots of people who like playing with words. They love words.

These people would be amused by this arrangement of letters:

K I N G

I D E A

N E X T

G A T E

The word lovers would call this a magic word square. Because words can be read across and down. From this pattern, you should be able to see that KING goes across and down. And also IDEA. And NEXT. And GATE.

Magic word squares aren't easy to make up, but it can be fun trying. In some ways, they can be more difficult to make than magic squares with numbers in.

Here is another magic square.

```
C O R E
O P E N
R E A D
E N D S
```

If you try and make up a magic word square, you don't have to have the same words going across as down. Here is a magic word square with different words across and down.

```
H A L E
E V E N
R I N D
O D D S
```

But this sort of magic word square is harder to make up than the sort where the same words go across and down.

Mental Arithmetic

You may not like arithmetic, especially mental arithmetic, but it is good exercise for your brain. Anyone with an alert brain ought to have no problems doing the few sums set out here. Test them on yourself. Sometimes it isn't even necessary to do all the working out involved. An alert brain will see short cuts and be able to go straight to the answer.

Here are the sums.

$2 + 2 = ?$

$3 + 3 + 3 = ?$

$4 + 4 + 4 + 4 = ?$

$5 + 5 + 5 + 5 + 5 = ?$

$1 + 2 + 3 + 4 + 5 = ?$

$2 + 4 + 6 + 8 + 10 = ?$

$4 + 8 + 12 + 16 + 20 = ?$

$1 \times 1 \times 1 \times 1 \times 1 \times 1 \times 1 = ?$

$1 \times 2 \times 3 \times 4 \times 5 \times 6 \times 7 \times 8 \times 9 \times 0 = ?$

Which of these was the easiest? And which was the hardest?

To give your brain a chance to do more exercises, you should make up your own sums. What sorts of sums are the most difficult? You should include some of that sort in the ones you make up.

Mind~bogglers

Difficult puzzles are sometimes called mind-bogglers – or brain-teasers.

Here are some mind-boggling questions. See how well you do with them.

Write down the number eleven thousand, eleven hundred, and eleven.

Write down eight eights so that they add up to exactly 1000.

What's the next number in this series?

$$8\ 5\ 4\ 9\ 1\ 7\ -$$

(The answer can only be between 1 and 10.)

Use up all of these letters, HIJKLMNO, to make a boy's name and the name of a drink.

How much dirt is there in a hole measuring 23 cm by $17\frac{1}{2}$ cm by $43\frac{1}{4}$ cm?

Which are there more of: inches in a mile or Sundays in a thousand years?

What word in the English language is always pronounced wrongly?

How many marbles can you put into an empty bag?

What's black and white and *red* all over? (Not a newspaper!)

Which are there more of: inches in three yards or weeks in three years?

Which is the bigger number: 1234 multiplied by 5678 or 2468 multiplied by 2468?

(You will find the answers at the back of the book.)

Names

You know what your name is. But have you ever stopped to think about it? Do you like it? Do you hate it? Lots of people don't like their names when they are young, but they tend not to mind so much as they get older.

Have you ever asked your Mum and Dad why they chose your name for you instead of some other name? Why did they choose the names that your brothers and sisters have got (assuming that you have some brothers and sisters)? Do your Mum and Dad like their own names?

If you could change your name, what would you like to be called? You wouldn't want the same name as your best friend, would you?

Hundreds of years ago, some of the names that were given to children were strange. Like Guinevere, Agnes and Lavinia, which are all girls' names. And Cuthbert, Archibald and Bertram, which are all boys' names. But times have changed.

Parents have thought up new names for children. Like Sharon and Tracy for girls. And Jason and Wayne for boys. There are some names which are always popular, like John, William, Richard, and Robert.

Make a list of the names of all the children in your class. Which names do you like? Which ones don't you like? And which ones are in between?

Make a list of all the names that you would like to be called, and a list of those that you wouldn't like to be called. Get your friends to do the same thing, then compare your lists. Has everyone chosen the same favourite names? Or do people's favourite names differ quite a lot?

Do you think that people's names suit them? Some

grown-ups have an idea that children grow up to suit their names. If a girl has a pleasant sounding name, she will grow up to be a nice pleasant grown-up. If a boy has a silly sounding name, he will grow up to be a rather silly grown-up. Do you think there is any truth in this? Or is it a silly idea?

Needs

When people need to think hard about a problem, they like to be alone sometimes. Or close their eyes. Or have silence all around them. That's because there is nothing else for their brain to think about. Apart from the problem.

Perhaps your Dad sometimes tells you to turn off the television. Not because he doesn't like the programme that's on, but because he doesn't want the noise or the picture to distract him while he is thinking.

Some people need to have some tea or coffee to drink. What do you need to help you think? Do you find that it's easier to think about things in certain places? Or at certain times of the day?

By knowing what you need when you think, you might be able to solve problems better. If you have a problem and you want to think about it, make sure that your needs are met. That you've got silence, or that you're alone, or that you've got a glass of lemon, or whatever it is that you need to help you think.

Numbers

Numbers are for counting things. For keeping track of things. If you start off with 25 pence in your pocket and then someone gives you 18 pence more, it's useful to know that you've now got 43 pence. You haven't just got some unknown amount of money. You've got 43 pence.

Numbers are useful for counting all sorts of things. Apples. Or books. Or chocolate sweets. Or dots on the ceiling. Or eggs in a box. And so on.

Numbers are a good way to exercise your brain. If your brain is nimble at handling numbers, good for you! If it isn't, you must make it familiar with numbers. Numbers are just one more way to get Brain Power!

Here are some number exercises. You can either do them in your head or you can use pencil and paper.

Add up all the numbers from 1 to 10.
What's half of 2 plus 4 plus 6 plus 8?

Can you double 3 plus 4 plus 5?

What is a quarter of 40?

If a packet of crisps cost 8 pence, how much do five packets cost?

Is 7 times 8 the same as 8 times 7?

How many times does 2 go into 20?

What is the largest number less than 100?

If a gross is another name for 144, how many make up half a gross?

Add together 1 and 11 and 21 and 31 and 41.

Add together $\frac{1}{2}$ and $1\frac{1}{2}$ and $2\frac{1}{2}$ and $3\frac{1}{2}$.

Add together $\frac{1}{3}$ and $\frac{1}{3}$ and $\frac{1}{3}$.

If you can do all of these without too much bother, make up your own sums. Try them on your friends. They need Brain Power as much as you do. Everyone needs Brain Power!

Outdoors

This is another of several exercises to see how well you observe the ordinary when you are out of doors. First, find a comfortable chair at home and finish reading about the exercises. Then go outdoors and try them.

Here are some questions about things that you might see while you are out walking. Walking to school. Walking to a friend's house. Walking to the shops. Try to answer them in your head. Then check as many as you can in the real world.

How many colours are there on traffic lights?
What are the colours?
Which colour is at the top?
Which way do you have to walk along your street for the house numbers to get higher?
Do the house numbers go up in ones or twos?
Where is the nearest telephone box to your home?
Where is the nearest post box to your home?
Are there telephone poles in your street?
Do buses travel along your road?

What colour are the buses?
Do you know where the nearest bus stop is?

Here are some more exercises. Try to imagine a walk that you've done lots of times. To school. To a friend's house. To the shops. Choose one of these walks. Now choose a colour. Make a list of all the things that you see on the walk that have that colour. Then go and check the list. Do this by walking to school, your friend's house, or the shops.

You might decide to choose the walk to school. And you might choose the colour blue. Your list of blue things that you would expect to see might include buses. And the milk van from the local dairy. And the nurses' dresses who work in the big hospital nearby. And the police cars that are always parked across the street. And lots more.

Here is another exercise. This is a good one to do with a friend. Choose a street that you both know well. Each of you must make a list of all the things in that street that you can think of. The houses. The shops. The other buildings. The trees. The telephone poles. The bus stops. Everything. Exchange lists, and see what your friend has put down that you missed out. Then the two of you should walk down the street and check your lists. Who got most right? Who missed most out?

P

People

How well do you know people around you? The people you meet or see every day. Or nearly every day.

Here are some questions.

Make a list of the left-handed people that you know. Check the names on the list when you next meet the people. Were you right?

Make a list of people who wear glasses. Every time you meet someone with glasses, check to see if they were on the list.

List all the grown-ups that you can think of at your school. The teachers, the librarian, the cleaners. Can you think of all of them? Making sure not to leave any of them out.

Can you describe your teachers? Or make a list of odd things that they do? Is there a man teacher who always brings an umbrella to school, even on sunny days? Is there a woman teacher who always wears the same shoes? Have you noticed other odd things about the teachers?

If you think it's a bit unfair to pick on your teachers like this, you're absolutely right! Try the same thing for your friends. And your parents. And other relations.

Possibilities

Possibilities are the things that are possible. They may not actually happen. But they could happen. They are possible.

For instance, imagine that you have arranged to meet a friend outside a public park at four o'clock on a Saturday afternoon. You arrive at the park in plenty of time. At a quarter to four. Your friend doesn't show up at four o'clock. Your friend hasn't arrived by five minutes past four. Fifteen more minutes go by. And still no sign of your friend. It's now half past four. And still no friend.

What thoughts are going through your mind? Probably the very worst ones! You might be thinking that your friend has had an accident.

But stop! Consider *all* the possibilities. Not just the nasty ones. Maybe you got the time wrong. Perhaps you agreed to meet your friend at five o'clock, not four o'clock. Are you absolutely sure about the time that you arranged to meet?

What about the place? Are you completely sure that it was this park that you were to meet at? Could it have been another one? Maybe your friend is at another park wondering where on earth you are!

Maybe your friend wasn't too sure where the park was. And then got slightly lost. Give him a few more minutes and he may turn up.

Maybe his father was going to give him a ride in the family car to get to the park. And perhaps the car broke down? Is that possible?

Maybe your friend was naughty and his mother wouldn't let him go out to the park. Is that possible? Does your friend often get stopped from going out like that?

Are you sure that you were to meet on Saturday? Could it have been Sunday? Or next Saturday even?

Run through all of the possibilities. However absurd some of them may seem. Then ask yourself how *likely* each one is. If your friend often turns up late, then it's quite likely he'll be late this time. If he only lives ten minutes' walk away from the park and his father's car broke down, he could have walked to the park quite quickly. It's not very likely that he won't have appeared by half past four. And so on.

Ask yourself what sort of things could have happened to you to make *you* late arriving at the park. Could they have happened to your friend?

Problems

Suppose you've got a problem. Sometimes it isn't enough to just know that you've got one. It often helps to know where it came from. And that's not always easy. Different problems occur in different ways.

Here is one way. You suspect that something isn't quite right. Not the way it should be. Not the way you're used to. The custard that your Mum gave you for tea was an odd colour. You switched on the television, and there was no picture or sound.

Here is another way. Someone brings a problem to you. They ask you to help with their problem. Suddenly, their problem has become your problem. Perhaps it's nine o'clock in the evening. Your younger sister wants some help with her homework. And she tells you that it's got to be ready for school early next morning. Her problem has suddenly become your problem.

Here is yet another way. Something has been bothering you for a while. You've tried ignoring it. You hoped that it would go away. But it hasn't. You're fed up with it bothering you. So you decide to do something about it at last. It could be that you lost a piece of a jigsaw set ages ago. You decided that you would use the jigsaw and make do without the piece that was missing. But it annoys you not having the piece. So, you decide that you will try really hard to find it.

One more way. You do something and all of a sudden you are in the middle of a problem. You were coming home from school. You left your bag outside the sweet shop while you went in to get some sweets. And you forgot to pick it up when you left the shop. It's now ten o'clock at night. It's raining. And you've only just remembered that you left your bag at the sweet shop.

Can you think of other ways in which problems appear? Can you think of other ways you've first noticed them?

Puzzles

Lots of grown-ups like puzzles. They know that they are a good way to keep their brains in training. The same goes for you. The puzzles here will make you think. They will make your brain do a bit more work than it's used to. Some of them have answers. And some of them don't. The sort that don't are there to make you think. It doesn't matter that there isn't a right answer. It's not the answer that's important. It's the thinking.

Here are the puzzles. Take your time over them.

The first puzzle. There were two brothers. They were called Reuben and Efrem. Reuben was ill in bed one morning. It was the first day of April. April Fool's Day. Efrem went into Reuben's bedroom. He said to Reuben, 'Today is April Fool's Day, Reuben, and I shall fool you as you have never been fooled before!' With that, Efrem left the room. Poor Reuben lay in bed all day long. He was waiting for Efrem to come in and fool him. He was wondering what Efrem might have in store for him. But Efrem never came back into Reuben's room. Late that night, Reuben's mother asked him, 'Why don't you go to sleep?' Reuben replied that he was waiting for Efrem to fool him. The mother turned to Efrem and said, 'Efrem, will you please fool Reuben, and then he can go to sleep!'

Efrem turned to Reuben. This is how the conversation went.
Efrem: You thought I was going to fool you, didn't you?
Reuben: Yes.
Efrem: But I didn't, did I?
Reuben: No.
Efrem: But you expected me to fool you, didn't you?
Reuben: Yes.
Efrem: So I fooled you after all, didn't I?

Poor Reuben. He lay there for much of the night.

He couldn't sleep. Had he really been fooled or not? If Reuben wasn't fooled, then he did not get what he expected. So he was fooled. That was Efrem's argument. But on the other hand, if Reuben was fooled, he did get what he expected. So in what way was Reuben fooled?

So, was Reuben fooled or not?

The second puzzle. Teachers do their best to try and get their pupils to speak and write properly. But how much of it sinks in? Do you know whether it is more correct to say the yolk of an egg *is* white or the yolk of an egg *are* white?

The third puzzle. If an aeroplane crashes right on the border of England and Scotland, which country should the survivors be buried in?

The fourth puzzle. A man was looking at a picture. Someone else came along. And they asked whose picture he was looking at. The man replied, 'Brothers and sisters have I none, but this man's father is my father's son.'

That might seem like a strange reply. After all, the man could have answered the question directly. But he didn't. Perhaps you can work out whose picture the man was looking at.

The fifth puzzle. Over a hundred years ago, the President of the United States of America was a very famous and very wise man called Abraham Lincoln. This was one of his favourite puzzles that he used to try on people. Here it is. If the tail of a dog was called a leg, how many legs would a dog really have?

The sixth puzzle. This puzzle was first devised by a man known as Lewis Carroll. He also wrote the stories about Alice in Wonderland and Alice through the Looking-glass. One of his favourite questions that he used to try on people was this one. Which is better, a clock that loses a minute a day or a clock that doesn't go at all? According to Lewis Carroll, the clock that doesn't go at all is a better clock because it shows the right time twice a day. (Think about it!) The other clock that loses a minute every day will only be right once in every *two years*. Do you agree with Lewis Carroll? Would you rather have a clock that didn't go at all? Or one that lost a minute every day?

Quick Thinking

This is an exercise that will speed up your brain. Get it working faster. But you do need to have a friend with you to play this game.

In this game, when the first player says 'One, two,

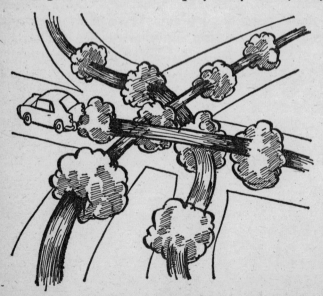

three, finger shoot!' the players each extend one or more fingers on one hand.

Both players must add up the total number of fingers extended and shout out the answer. The winner scores one point. But only if he's got the *right* answer.

There are lots of ways to make the game harder. And these are all good ways of making your brain concentrate.

Here are some of the other ways.

Both players can use two hands.

The numbers of fingers have to be multiplied together instead of added together.

Three or even more players can play.

Quizzes

A quiz is a list of questions. Questions about all sorts of things. Sometimes you will know the answers. Sometimes you might have to look up the answers in a book. And sometimes you will be totally stuck. Quizzes are to make you think. If you think you know the answer, fine! If you think you don't know the answer, the next step is to start thinking how you would go about finding out the answer.

Here are some quiz questions. See how many of them you can get answers for. Whether you know the answers straightaway. Or whether you have to look them up in a book.

What is the largest city in England?
What country is joined to England at its western side?
What country is joined to England at its northern side?
What is the name of the nearest star in the sky?
What is the name of the Queen of Great Britain?
Do you know who Charlie Chaplin was?
Do you know who William Shakespeare was?

Once you've answered these quiz questions, you could make up your own. Get together with some friends. Each of you should make a list of ten questions. See if you can answer the questions on each other's lists. If you have any troubles answering a particular question, don't just give up. Make every effort to find out. Look in books. Ask your teachers. Ask your parents. Even if they tell you the answer straightaway, it will still be good practice for you to ask the question.

R

Reading

The earlier you learn to read the better. The more you read the better. Comics, short stories, story books, road signs, labels on bottles of tomato ketchup. All sorts of things. Reading will introduce you to lots of new words. And lots of new ideas.

If you come across a word that you don't recognise, ask someone. Find out what it means. Don't skip over it, hoping that it won't appear again. Words do reappear. They keep coming back. Don't be afraid to ask. Find out what the word is, and what it means. Find out how to use it yourself.

Get to know how to use a dictionary. Look up the words you don't fully understand.

Here are some words for you to look up. If they aren't in the dictionary you use, ask someone if you can try another dictionary.

The words: Kangaroo. Bureau. Sash. Vinegar. Ostrich. Committee. Harp. Harpoon. Walrus. Pelmet.

Surname. Gallon. Jester. Channel. Magnolia. Enigma. Lacrosse.

Real Things

This game will test your sense of taste. You will need some small pieces of food that are all crunchy. Like a raw potato, a carrot, an onion, an apple, and so on. You'll also need a friend to help you.

One of you needs to close your eyes and hold your nose. The other one should put a piece of one of the foods in your mouth. Guess which one it is.

Try this for several different foods. Then switch round so that the one that did the tasting is now putting food in the other's mouth.

Try it with creamy things, too. Like cold custard, blancmange, milk jelly, cream, cold mashed potato, ice cream, and so on.

You don't have to stay with foods, either. You could use things that you drink. Like milk, lemonade, orange juice, cola, water, and so on. Different flavoured milk shakes might be useful, too.

Is your taste linked more to your sight or smell? Can you feel the differences between things with only your sense of taste?

Riddles

Everyone knows what a riddle is. It's a silly question where you have to try and work out the silly answer! Like this: When is a door not a door? When it's a jar!

Riddles are fun. But riddles are another good way of exercising your brain. What makes a riddle a riddle? Why is a riddle silly? Why is the answer silly?

If you can think about riddles and see why they are silly, you can have a laugh and exercise your brain at the same time! And doing two things at once is usually quite clever!

Here are some riddles and their answers. What makes them silly?

Why are a star and an old barn alike?
Because they both contain r-a-t-s.

Where are queens usually crowned?
On the head.

What did the rug say to the floor?
Hands up, I've got you covered.

Why is an empty purse always the same?
Because there's never any change in it.

Why is a dog's tail like the heart of a tree?
Because it's furthest from the bark.

What are the largest ants?
Gi-ants.

Why isn't your nose twelve inches long?
Because if it were it would be a foot.

Routes

A route is the way that you get from one place to another place. There will be a route for you to get from your home to your school. There will be a route to get from your home to your best friend's home. There are lots of routes, to and from all sorts of different places. There doesn't have to be just one route between two places. If you decided to go to school in a different way one morning, you would be taking a different route. There can be lots of routes between the same two places.

Can you describe the route that you take to get from home to school? Imagine that you had to tell someone else how to get from your home to your school. They've never been to your home before. Or your school. Can you tell them exactly what to do once they've left your home? Which way should they turn? Left or right? How far should they walk? And then which way should they turn? And how will they know when they've reached your school?

Write out the route that you take to get to school. Check it tomorrow (or the next time you go to school). Is it right? Have you left out anything?

Maps. A map is a picture which shows you where different places are. You may have seen all sorts of maps in different books.

Maybe the book you were reading last week had a map of a treasure island. The map showed where the treasure was buried. And where the pirate's cave was. And where the river was that ran down to the sea.

Maybe you've seen the map that your Dad keeps in the car showing him where all the villages and towns and cities in the country are.

Or maybe you've seen a map of the world, showing all the continents and countries and oceans.

Maps are useful for letting you work out your own route from one place to another place. When visitors come to your home, they don't always need route instructions to get there. If you just tell them the address and they have a map, they ought to be able to work out the route for themselves. Wherever they start from doesn't matter to you. The route is up to them. You have told them where you live. They look at the map. They decide how to get from their starting place to your home.

Why not try to draw a map of your town, showing your home and your friends' homes and your school? Mark the main shops and parks. Mark any rivers or streams. Connect them all up with the roads that run between them all. Try and mark as many different places as you can think of on your map.

5

Situations

How good are you at finding your way out of perplexing situations? Here are some situations. See
how you deal with them.

The first one. You have a can full right up to the
brim with orange juice. You take the plastic lid off
the can. Then you find that you have got nothing to
drink from except the can. With nothing available

for measuring the depth of the can or its contents, how do you share it with a friend so that each of you gets exactly half the orange juice?

The second one. It is impossible to place four pebbles on a table so that each is exactly the same distance from all the other three. But it can be done on a sandy beach. How?

The third one. You are on the rocky shore of a desert island. You find a little fresh water that has collected in a small depression in a rock. Your only utensil is a spoon. And the depression is too deep for you to scoop up the water with the spoon. Also, the handle of the spoon is too strong for you to bend it at all. How can you scoop the water out of the hole?

Sleep

There are some problems which will completely baffle you. You have no ideas at all. Not even wrong ideas!

Inspiration is what you need. Something to give you a start. A push in the right direction. A new angle.

At times like this, the best solution might be to go to sleep. Sleep on the problem. Don't lie awake all night thinking about it. Let it churn around in your brain while you are asleep. Even when you are sleeping, the brain works on. It might be that during the night your brain manages to think of a new angle on the problem. When you wake up in the morning the new approach suddenly presents itself to you.

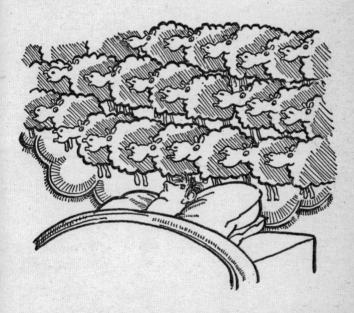

You might be surprised. It might be just what you needed to get a grasp on the problem. On the other hand, it might not work at all. It's not a guaranteed method. It just works for some people sometimes. And if you're having problems getting to sleep, you need something to distract your attention from the problem. You could count sheep. But that's a bit boring and old-fashioned. And it's so easy, you will probably find yourself counting sheep and concentrating on your problem at the same time.

What you need to do is concentrate on something else. So try this exercise.

Run through the alphabet thinking of a famous person whose name begins with each letter. When you get to Z, go back to the beginning. But don't use the same names the second time through. Keep thinking of new names. Your brain will become so tired of trying to remember whether you have already used a name or not that you will eventually doze off. Here is an example. A is for Anne Boleyn, B is for Boris Karloff, C is for Cary Grant, and D is for Doris Day. If you don't know who these people are, it doesn't matter. Just use the names of people that you know about.

T

Thinking

This is what Brain Power is all about. Thinking. Thinking in new ways. Thinking in different ways. Thinking in old ways with new twists. Think, think, think!

But you need lots of practice. And that's what this book is providing. Practice. And exercises. And tests. And things to do. To give you Brain Power.

Sometimes the problem isn't even looking at something in a new way. Maybe the problem is that you actually expect to see a certain something. And whether it's really there or not, that's what you end up seeing. Not good enough! You must look carefully.

Try these:

> Lots and lots of thinking is
> is just what your brain needs.

> What do you think might be
> be wrong with this sentence?

Do you usually make the
the same mistake twice?

Do be careful and do
do look at things twice.

Sometimes there just isn't enough information to be
sure about what you think. Perhaps you think that
thinking anything is going to be a waste of time
until you get more information.

But let your mind run free! What might be the
missing information? If it was one thing, what
would you think then? How would what you were
thinking change if your guess about the missing information was wrong? Even before you've got the
missing information, think of the possibilities. Then
when you've got the information, everything might
drop neatly into place.

Tongue Twisters

Everyone knows what a tongue twister is. It's a
fiendish saying that people have problems with
when they try to say it fast. And if they try to repeat
it several times and say it fast, they run into even
more problems!

Even a simple phrase like 'Red lorry, yellow lorry'
repeated over and over will get your tongue in a

twist. Another simple one is 'Red leather, yellow leather'. Try saying these over and over quickly. You're bound to get muddled up!

But why are tongue twisters tongue twisters? What is it about them that makes them difficult?

Here are some more tongue twisters. Can you decide why they are tongue twisters?

One wins well when young.
Three thrushes settle on three thistles.
Four fat friars fried frankfurters.
The sixth sheik's sixth sheep's sick!
Eleven elephants left eleven lots of elevenses.
Fifteen fluffy feathers fell from feeble Fifi's fan.
If twenty tinkers took twenty-two tacks to Tooting, how many tacks did the twenty tinkers take to Totton?

True or False ?

Sometimes it's difficult to work out just what is true and what isn't. Even when you have all the information which you need. You feel as if your brain's getting twisted up somehow.

Is the sentence below true or false?

THIS SENTENCE IS FALSE.

If it is false, then it is true. And if it is true, then it is false. What does your brain make of that? Can it be sorted out? Is it really true? Or really false? Or is it neither? Is it possible to have something which is neither true nor false? Would it make sense?

Here is another problem, somewhat similar. Imagine that you have a plain postcard. It doesn't have a picture on either side. On one side is written the following sentence:

THE SENTENCE ON THE OTHER SIDE OF THIS CARD IS TRUE.

Then you turn the card over. On the other side is written this sentence:

THE SENTENCE ON THE OTHER SIDE OF THIS CARD IS FALSE.

If the first sentence is true, then the second sentence must be true. Because the first sentence says so. But the second sentence says the first sentence is false. And if the first sentence is false, then the second sentence is false. So the first sentence is not false but true. So the first sentence is only true if it is false. And that *is* impossible!

What's going on here? Can your brain come to grips with this? How can two such simple sentences written down on a postcard cause such confusion? Don't get too worried if your brain can't unravel this one.

Lots of the world's greatest thinkers have struggled with problems like these. In an attempt to understand how people think. How their brains work. And what true and false really mean. Their thoughts about this problem are very long and very involved. And they don't all manage to convince each other that what they've thought is correct. Perhaps this is one time when you should give your brain a rest!

U

Uses

This is another of the exercises to get your brain thinking in new directions. Thinking of the odd, the strange, the unusual.

You have got to make up some lists of things you could do with things you know. And there's a time limit of three minutes for each list. See how many uses you can think of.

List all the uses that could be made of an empty bottle.
List all the ways that you could earn money from your neighbours.
List all the uses that you can think of for a small bucket.
List all the things you could do with a piece of string three metres (ten feet) long.
List all the things you do with a large piece of green plasticine.

Now try the same exercises but with a time limit of ten minutes on each one. How many more things can you add to each list? It's easy to put down the first few things on each list. But it gets harder putting down the *last* few things. Unless your brain is very well trained!

U

Variety

A famous poet called William Cowper once wrote 'Variety's the very spice of life'. What did he mean by that?

The more things you know about, or read about, or understand, or think about, the more you will enjoy life. The more games you can play. The more books

you've read. The more people you know. The more different foods you've tried. The more places you've been.

If you only ever read one book, or ate one sort of food, or met just one person, wouldn't that be boring?

What makes life so wonderful is doing all the different things that can be done, going to all the different places that can be visited, thinking all the different thoughts that can be thought, and so on.

This book is trying to make you think in all sorts of different ways, rather than just thinking in one very boring way. This book is suggesting lots of things for you to do, lots of things for you to think about, lots of things to investigate. Brain Power is helped by having variety.

What Comes Next?

Here are some push-ups for your brain. Something for it to get to work on.

These first ones are easy, just to get you used to the idea. What comes next in each of these?

A B C D E F — — —

A B A C A D A — — —

A C E G I K — — —

A D G J M P — — —

Do you get the idea? Here come some more. Only they're not quite so easy. The answers are sensible when you see them. But you might not see them straightaway.

O T T F F S S E — — —

M T W T F — —

J F M A M J J A — — —

If you manage to get the right answers for all of

these (and you can check them out at the back of the book), why not try making up some of your own? Then try them on your friends. Which people come up with the answers immediately? And which ones have to think for ages?

What's Going On?

Get hold of some magazines and newspapers with lots of pictures in. The more pictures the better. Look at the pictures in turn. But don't read the words that go with the pictures. Try to work out what's going on in each of the pictures. Try to make a list of all the things that are happening. Or could be happening.

After you've tried working out what's happening in the pictures, read the words with the picture. How close were you? Were your guesses fairly accurate? Or were they way out?

What was special about the newspapers and magazines that had pictures that you were good at guessing at? Was there anything special about the newspapers and magazines where the pictures fooled you?

Did pictures with people in work better? Or worse? Did it help if it was a coloured picture? Or did it make no difference to you?

What's Wrong?

Which is better, happiness that lasts for ever and ever or a ham sandwich?

Your first answer is probably that happiness that lasts for ever and ever is much better than a ham sandwich. But this just isn't so! Let's see how this can be.

Nothing is better than happiness that lasts for ever and ever. And a ham sandwich is certainly better than nothing. So a ham sandwich must be better than happiness that lasts for ever and ever.

Does that seem logical? There must be something wrong there? Because everyone *knows* that happiness that lasts for ever and ever has got to be much better than a mouldy old ham sandwich! So what's gone wrong with the logic here?

Here's another one.

Count all of the fingers and thumbs on your two hands. How many? Ten. Now hold up one hand. Start counting the fingers and thumb backwards. Start at 10, then 9, 8, 7 and 6. Stop there. Now hold up the other hand. That's got four fingers and a thumb. 6 and 5 is eleven. So you must have eleven fingers and thumbs. Where did the extra one come from?

Words

Words are used to describe ideas. And thoughts. If you can't use words properly, you are going to have problems getting your ideas and thoughts across to other people. And the whole point of this book is to help you develop Brain Power. To solve problems. Or even to avoid having them at all.

The better you are with words, the less problems you will have. And you'll be able to sort out the ones you do have more quickly.

The English language is full of words. Lots and lots of different words. Lots of them mean the same thing. Lots of them mean almost the same thing. But not quite.
Here are some words that all mean roughly the same as 'idea':

Notion, thought, concept, theory, precept, image, belief, opinion.

And here are some words that all mean roughly the same as 'problem':

Difficulty, poser, stumper, enigma, mystery, teaser, intricacy, brain-twister.

Now here are some exercises for you to tackle. See how many words you can think of that mean the same as each of the words in this list.

The list:

Message, student, ask, go, help, put, hope, pause, throw, play, fight.

X is for the Unknown

Lots of people use the letter X to stand for something that is unknown. They often say that X stands for the unknown. Even though unknown begins with the letter U. That's just a thing that people say. And they've probably forgotten why they do say it!

People tend to be frightened of the unknown. If they don't know about something they try to avoid it. Which is silly. So they go on being frightened of it.

Some people are frightened of sums. But that's only because no-one ever properly explained to them all about sums. How to do them. Why they need to be done. How to get the right answers. They're only frightened of them because they are something unknown.

Other people are frightened of water. They don't like going near swimming pools. Or rivers. Or the sea. Usually these people can't swim. No-one ever taught them how. So water remains an unknown to them. They are frightened of water because no-one has ever taken the trouble to show them how to swim.

This fear of the unknown applies to all sorts of other things. But don't let it get to you.

If you are frightened of something, ask yourself why. Is it because you don't really understand it? Like history. Or telling the time. Or reading a map. Or is it something that you are frightened of because it could do you harm? Like that vicious dog that lives next door. Or lorries in the street outside.

Once you know why you are frightened of something, you can learn to deal with it. Lots of things will become less frightening. Other things will still be just as frightening as they ever were. But once you understand why that is so, you won't be so worried by the fact that you are frightened.

Yourself

How much do you really know about yourself? If you don't know about yourself, how on earth can you manage to come to grips with everyone else and everything else in the world?

Without looking, what colour socks have you got on? Now look and check.

When you fold your arms (no, don't do it yet!), one hand is on top and the other is tucked in. Do you know which is which for you? Guess first. Then try it and see.

When you get dressed in the morning, do you put on your left shoe or your right shoe first? And which one do you take off first? The same one? Or the other one? Check and see tomorrow.

When you clasp your hands together, which thumb is on top? Guess. Then try it.

If you had to use a telescope, which eye would you

use? Your right eye? Or your left eye? If you don't have a telescope to try this with, use an empty cardboard tube instead.

There are all sorts of things about yourself that you don't know. How can you go through life not really knowing yourself? This has got to stop! You must wake up! Shake some life into your brain! Stop drifting through every day in a haze about yourself!

There must be all sorts of other things that you really don't know about yourself. How long will it take you to think of them?

2

Zany Tales

By now, your brain should be quite well trained. It ought to be thinking carefully about problems. About situations. About odd events. And about everyday events. If you've read all of the book this far and done the exercises, you've probably developed a lot of Brain Power. Let's see.

Here are two short stories which seem a bit zany. But only at first. If you think about them, you should see that they are not so zany after all. Can you explain them?

First story.

A man went for a walk. It started to rain. It poured down. He didn't have a hat. And he'd forgotten his umbrella. His clothes got completely soaked. His shoes got wet and began to let in the rain. But not a hair on his head got wet. How come?

And the second story.

Percy, Martha, Boris and Sarah live in the same house. One night, Percy and Martha went out to the cinema. When they arrived back home later on, they found Sarah lying dead on the floor. But Boris wasn't arrested. He wasn't even questioned for any crime! Why not?

Answers

Anagrams

Mile, acts and cast, ales and sale, army, able, blot, acre and race, edit and tide and tied, eats and sate and seat and teas. Chase, agree, alter, range, boats, dance, freed, wrong, earth.

Deductions

Kevin is happy.
Some dreams are both terrible and in colour.
My sisters cannot sing.
Grown-ups cannot sit still.
No cats can whistle.

Differences

One sells tea sets, the other sells settees.
One minds the train, the other trains the mind.
Fleas can't have elephants on them.
Killed soldiers are dead men, repaired clothes are men-ded.
One knows his blows, the other blows his nose.
One is a mad bunny, the other is bad money.
One baits his hook, the other hates his book.
One eats too long, the other longs to eat.
One is difficult to get up, the other is difficult to get down.

Letters

To read CHECKED, CHOICE and so on, turn the page upside down and look at it in a mirror.

Logic

A donkey.

Snorters.

Magic Squares

The missing numbers are 7 in the second row, 10 in the third row, and 3 in the fourth row.

Mental Arithmetic

4
9
16
25
15
30
60
1
0

Mind-bogglers

12, 111.
888+88+8+8+8 = 1000.
6 (the names of the numbers are written in alpha-betical order).
John and milk.
None.
Inches in a mile.
Wrongly.
One (it's not empty after that).
An embarrassed zebra!
Inches in 3 yards.
1234 multiplied by 5678.

Numbers

55
10
18
10
40p
Yes, 56
10 times
99
72
105
8
1

Puzzles

Yes.
The yolk of an egg is yellow, not white!
You don't bury the survivors anywhere!
His son.
Four legs (whatever you call its tail, it's still only got four legs.)

Thinking

The words 'is', 'be', 'the', and 'do' are all repeated.

What Comes Next?
GHI.
EAF.
MOQ.
SVY.
NTE (initial letters of the numbers: one, two, three, . . .)
TF (initial letters of the days: Monday, Tuesday, . . .)
SON (initial letters of the months: January, February, March, . . .)

Zany Tales

1st Story: The man was completely bald and didn't have a hair on his head.
2nd Story: Boris was a cat, and Sarah was a goldfish.